Sammy Sloth

The 'Get to Know Me' series is aimed at children with additional needs and those who support them in the classroom. Developed by child psychologist Dr Louise Lightfoot and illustrated by Catherine Hicks, the resources in this series include activities specific to anxiety, depression and Obsessive Compulsive Disorder (OCD). This book, *Sammy Sloth*, has been designed to support the individual child but also to be used in whole class teaching, to encourage an empathetic and inclusive environment.

In this book, we meet Sammy, a sloth who lives in a beautiful tree by the sea. The story follows Sammy as he wakes up one day to find he feels funny and strange. He can't sit still and does not feel like his usual happy and relaxed self. After pacing up and down he meets Anna the Armadillo who tells Sammy that he is silly and has no right to be sad when his life is good. Sammy hears this and feels embarrassed and ashamed of how he has been feeling. Sammy hides away until he meets a kind lizard who shows him kindness and empathy.

This book was written with children with anxiety in mind, providing an opportunity to relate to Sammy's thoughts, feelings, behaviours and experiences. However, children with a range of needs may benefit from the story. The book is written in a narrative style, so it does not use diagnostic labels and is not intended for this purpose. Instead the focus is on creating a common language which children can understand and use to make sense of how they are feeling.

A practitioner guidebook (ISBN 978-0-8153-4941-9) and draw along version (ISBN 978-0-8153-4942-6) are also available.

Dr Louise Lightfoot is an Educational and Child Psychologist working with children and young people aged 0–25. She holds a BA in Educational Studies, MEd in the Psychology of Education and doctorate in Educational and Child Psychology. Louise has worked in a variety of settings ranging from mainstream schools to secure units and psychiatric facilities, and has a special interest in working to empower at risk or 'hard to reach' groups. As a person who suffers with Ehlers Danlos, stroke and dyslexia, she has a first-hand understanding of the frustrations and difficulties that accompany a specific physical or learning difficulty. Louise currently works as an HCPC registered Independent Psychologist. If you would like to discuss working with her, please contact Louise at: louise.lightfoot@hotmail.co.uk.

Catherine Hicks is an East Yorkshire artist, illustrator, wife and mother. She spent 13 years as a Registered Veterinary Nurse before injury and chronic illnesses led to her creative hobby becoming therapy. When Catherine and Louise were introduced, it was obvious they were kindred spirits and from there the Get to Know Me Series was born.

GET TO KNOW ME SERIES

Series author: Dr Louise Lightfoot
Illustrated by: Catherine Hicks

The **'Get to Know Me'** series is a series of resources aimed at children with additional needs and the professionals who support them in the mainstream primary classroom. Each resource concentrates on a different condition and comprises of three titles, available separately.

A **traditional children's picture book** – designed to support the individual child but also to be used in whole class teaching, to encourage an empathetic and inclusive environment.

An **interactive workbook**. This is a workbook version of the story in which individual children are encouraged to interact with the story in a creative way – through writing, drawing, scrap booking, collage, activities etc. (templates and cut outs will be made available online). Children are more likely to understand and process information if they have had to actively engage with it. The workbook will aid long-term recall and increase the level of understanding.

A **practitioner guide** created for key adults (teachers, therapists and parents) by a child psychologist, with activities specific to each condition. These activities will link to the books and offer practical tools and strategies to support the child and those around them in addition to the information specific to the condition to improve understanding of a child's needs to promote empathy and acceptance.

https://www.routledge.com/Get-To-Know-Me/book-series/GKM

Books included in this series:

Set 1 Get to Know Me: Anxiety
Available as a set and individual books

Book 1
Supporting Children with Anxiety to Understand and Celebrate Difference
A Get to Know Me Workbook and Guide for Parents and Practitioners
PB 978-0-8153-4941-9
eBook 978-1-351-16492-4

Book 2
Sammy Sloth
Get to Know Me: Anxiety
PB 978-0-8153-4953-2
eBook 978-1-351-16452-8

Book 3
Draw Along With Sammy Sloth
Get to Know Me: Anxiety
PB 978-0-8153-4942-6
eBook 978-1-351-16484-9

Set 2 Get to Know Me: Depression
Available as a set and individual books

Book 1
Supporting Children with Depression to Understand and Celebrate Difference
A Get to Know Me Workbook and Guide for Parents and Practitioners
PB 978-0-8153-4943-3
eBook 978-1-351-16480-1

Book 2
Silver Matilda
Get to Know Me: Depression
PB 978-0-8153-4945-7
eBook 978-1-351-16476-4

Book 3
Draw Along With Silver Matilda
Get to Know Me: Depression
PB 978-0-8153-4946-4
eBook 978-1-351-16472-6

Set 3 Get to Know Me: OCD
Available as a set and individual books

Book 1
Supporting Children with OCD to Understand and Celebrate Difference
A Get to Know Me Workbook and Guide for Parents and Practitioners
PB 978-0-8153-4948-8
eBook 978-1-351-16468-9

Book 2
Tidy Tim
Get to Know Me: OCD
PB 978-0-8153-4950-1
eBook 978-1-351-16460-3

Book 3
Draw Along With Tidy Tim
Get to Know Me: OCD
PB 978-0-8153-4951-8
eBook 978-1-351-16456-6

SAMMY SLOTH

GET TO KNOW ME: ANXIETY

DR LOUISE LIGHTFOOT

ILLUSTRATED BY CATHERINE HICKS

Routledge
Taylor & Francis Group

LONDON AND NEW YORK

First published 2020
by Routledge
2 Park Square, Milton Park, Abingdon, Oxon OX14 4RN

and by Routledge
52 Vanderbilt Avenue, New York, NY 10017

Routledge is an imprint of the Taylor & Francis Group, an informa business

British Library Cataloguing-in-Publication Data
A catalogue record for this book is available from the British Library

Library of Congress Cataloging-in-Publication Data
A catalog record has been requested for this book

ISBN: 978-0-8153-4953-2 (pbk)
ISBN: 978-1-315-16452-8 (ebk)

Typeset in Stone Informal
by Apex CoVantage, LLC

Series webpage https://www.routledge.com/Get-To-Know-Me/book-series/GKM

DEDICATIONS

From Louise:

To all the children in my life. I've tried to wangle you in somewhere but if your name doesn't rhyme very easily or your book never comes out it doesn't mean I don't love you!

To my nieces Freya and Livy, my nephews Jayden and Zack and my godchildren Maddie, Joni and Emily, Auntie Lou Lou loves you very much.

To the children of all of my friends and family, and those who I have been privileged enough to work with, you have taught me so much.

To all the Sams in my life – one special little boy, one bearded man, the Sam who taught me every little helps and one Zebra – ta-da!

From Catherine:

To my husband Owen and my kids, Erin and Drew. They are my world, my biggest fans and harshest critics. I couldn't have managed this without them. xx

CONTENTS

ACKNOWLEDGEMENTS

To Katrina my editor, thank you for taking a chance and sticking with us, especially during our particularly 'imperfectly flawed' moments! You have been a wonderful source of personal support and a professional wisdom.

Professor Kevin Woods for your (I often wondered if misguided) belief in me and continued support. Here's to being a square peg in a round hole.

The University of Manchester and the students of the Doctorate of Educational Psychology Course, in particular Jill and Ben Simpson, for their collaboration, perspective and belief.

Huge thank you for the contributions of: Dr Lindsay 'grammar' Kay, Dr Katie Pierce, Dr Richard Skelton, Dr Rachael Hornsby, Dr Rachel Lyons and Jade Charelson for their professional insight, unwavering friendship, invaluable contribution and time. You really are the Waitrose of Psychologists (quality wise, not overpriced!).

Thank you to all my family and friends who have endured numerous versions of these books and for their support during the periods in which I was very ill and gained tenacity from believing I could make something good come out of it all.

To Erin and Drew for being excellent guinea pigs and the source of great inspiration. To Owen for being a friend to me at 13 and 35 with admittedly slightly improved cooking skills. To Dianne Davies for her experience, support and knowledge of the area which helped more than you could know.

Thanks to Catherine Hicks, my illustrator, the gin to my tonic! Perhaps in finding each other we made two slightly broken people whole.

To Jenni O'Sullivan-Ward, Isabella Hickling and Sharon Pellegrini for all your last-minute help!

Thanks to Dr Paula Muir for your insight, guidance and Kefir.

A huge thank you to Tim Watson for your supervision, guidance and support. You have helped me realise my potential when I couldn't see it in myself. You are an excellent critical friend, fountain of knowledge and all round lovely person!

Thanks for my Dad for always believing in me and constantly filling my freezer and thanks to my big brother John, who annoyed me as a child and who has always been there for me as an adult.

To the Hickling family, I couldn't have wished to marry into a better family, your support love and acceptance of me as a Scouser is forever appreciated.

Thank you to Jonathan Merrett, the copy editor, for his patience and flexibility and to Leah Burton, my Editorial Assistant, for her help along the way.

Finally, a huge thank you to Gillian Steadman, my Senior Production Editor, who is the yin to my yang. Couldn't have done this without you!

Sammy Sloth – A picture book story

A sloth called Sammy
Lived in a tree
In a faraway land
Overlooking the sea.

He spent happy days
Climbing up trees
Enjoying the sun
And the cool evening breeze.

Sammy was happy
In his beautiful home;
He had family and friends
And was never alone.

Then one morning he woke
Feeling all funny,
With ants in his pants
And a knot in his tummy.

He couldn't keep still,
Like he drank too much pop,
Thoughts rushed round his head
And they just wouldn't stop!

He felt whizzy and fizzy
And tizzy inside,
And he couldn't relax
Though he really tried.

So he paced up and down
Till it made his feet ache,
But he didn't feel tired
He felt wide awake.

So he climbed down the tree
And sat on a stone.
"Get off me!" he heard.
He wasn't alone.

He'd found Anna the Armadillo,
He'd sat down on her shell.
"I'm sorry" said Sammy,
"I don't feel too well."

"Whatever's the matter
Why can't you sit still?
Watching you pace
Is making me ill!

"I thought sloths were slow,
They don't rush around,
They're still and they chill
And they generally lounge."

"I was slow," said Sammy.
"But there was a change
And now I feel buzzy
And fuzzy and strange."

"You must know what's wrong,
So fix it today.
So stop with the worry
And you'll be ok."

"But that's just the problem,
I don't really know.
Nothing has happened
For my worries to grow."

Anna looked puzzled.
"That sounds silly to me.
You have plenty to eat
And your very own tree.

"You have family and friends
And a place to belong;
And you lie in sun
So what could be wrong?"

Then Sammy felt silly,
As that was all true.
And shame filled his heart,
What was he to do?

So he climbed up the tree
And tried to forget
The knot in his tummy
That was making him fret.

And he tried to sit still
But more thoughts whizzed about.
"But everything's fine!"
He heard himself shout.

"If you don't mind me saying,
Things don't look fine.
The fact you're shouting
Is not a good sign."

Livy the Lizard
Had heard Sammy shout.
"It's ok to be mad
Just let it out!"

"But that's just the problem,"
Sammy replied.
"I just can't calm down
I can't stop the wiggly feelings inside.

"And Anna was right,
I've a wonderful life,
And so many others
Face hardship and strife."

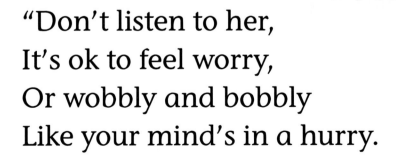

"Don't listen to her,
It's ok to feel worry,
Or wobbly and bobbly
Like your mind's in a hurry.

"And sometimes our worries
Are big or they're small
But sometimes we worry
For no reason at all.

"We might have a problem
The needs to be solved
And this can upset us
Until it's resolved.

"And sometimes the small things
We worry about
Can build up and up
Until it they burst out!

"And sometimes for reasons
We cannot explain,
We feel different inside
Although things look the same.

"But whatever the reason
You must never feel shame
Or guilty or silly
Or that you are to blame.

"What you need is a friend
To help you find out
What makes you feel better
And be there throughout.

"And whatever that is
We can do it together.
And remember these feelings
Won't last forever.

"I'm happy to listen
If you want to talk
Or I'll sit beside you
Or go for a walk.

"I don't know your troubles
Or why they have grown,
But I know you no longer
Must face them alone."

Sammy Sloth – text only version

A sloth called Sammy
Lived in a tree
In a faraway land
Overlooking the sea.

He spent happy days
Climbing up trees
Enjoying the sun
And the cool evening breeze.

Sammy was happy
In his beautiful home;
He had family and friends
And was never alone.

Then one morning he woke
Feeling all funny,
With ants in his pants
And a knot in his tummy.

He couldn't keep still,
Like he drank too much pop,
Thoughts rushed round his head
And they just wouldn't stop!

He felt whizzy and fizzy
And tizzy inside,
And he couldn't relax
Though he really tried.

So he paced up and down
Till it made his feet ache,
But he didn't feel tired
He felt wide awake.

So he climbed down the tree
And sat on a stone.
"Get off me!" he heard.
He wasn't alone.

He'd found Anna the Armadillo,
He'd sat down on her shell.
"I'm sorry" said Sammy,
"I don't feel too well."

"Whatever's the matter
Why can't you sit still?
Watching you pace
Is making me ill!

"I thought sloths were slow,
They don't rush around,
They're still and they chill
And they generally lounge."

"I was slow," said Sammy.
"But there was a change
And now I feel buzzy
And fuzzy and strange."

"You must know what's wrong,
So fix it today.
So stop with the worry
And you'll be ok."

"But that's just the problem,
I don't really know.
Nothing has happened
For my worries to grow."

Anna looked puzzled.
"That sounds silly to me.
You have plenty to eat
And your very own tree.

"You have family and friends
And a place to belong;
And you lie in sun
So what could be wrong?"

Then Sammy felt silly,
As that was all true.
And shame filled his heart,
What was he to do?

So he climbed up the tree
And tried to forget
The knot in his tummy
That was making him fret.

And he tried to sit still
But more thoughts whizzed about.
"But everything's fine!"
He heard himself shout.

"If you don't mind me saying,
Things don't look fine.
The fact you're shouting
Is not a good sign."

Livy the Lizard
Had heard Sammy shout.
"It's ok to be mad
Just let it out!"

"But that's just the problem,"
Sammy replied.
"I just can't calm down
I can't stop the wiggly feelings inside.

"And Anna was right,
I've a wonderful life,
And so many others
Face hardship and strife."

"Don't listen to her,
It's ok to feel worry,
Or wobbly and bobbly
Like your mind's in a hurry.

"And sometimes our worries
Are big or they're small
But sometimes we worry
For no reason at all.

"We might have a problem
The needs to be solved
And this can upset us
Until it's resolved.

"And sometimes the small things
We worry about
Can build up and up
Until it they burst out!

"And sometimes for reasons
We cannot explain,
We feel different inside
Although things look the same.

"But whatever the reason
You must never feel shame
Or guilty or silly
Or that you are to blame.

"What you need is a friend
To help you find out
What makes you feel better
And be there throughout.

"And whatever that is
We can do it together.
And remember these feelings
Won't last forever.

"I'm happy to listen
If you want to talk
Or I'll sit beside you
Or go for a walk.

"I don't know your troubles
Or why they have grown,
But I know you no longer
Must face them alone."